CALEDONIAN — The Monster

Guthrie Hutton

It was hoped that the canal would assist the Navy in the wars with France in the early nineteenth century, but it was not until the First World War that its usefulness in wartime was put to the test. The canal may have helped the Navy, but since the Navy paid no dues the increased traffic did not help the canal.

First published in the United Kingdom, 1992,
second edition published 2009
by Stenlake Publishing Ltd.
www.stenlake.co.uk
ISBN 9781840334500

Gondolier was the best known of the canal paddle steamers. Here she is being worked down the lock flight at Fort Augustus early this century. Fort Augustus is the only town of any substance between Inverness and Banavie, so the time taken in the locks gave passengers a welcome break ashore, to stretch their legs and spend their money.

FURTHER READING

Jean Lindsay, *The Canals of Scotland*, 1968.
A.D. Cameron, *The Caledonian Canal*, 1983.
A.D. Cameron, *Getting to know .. The Caledonian Canal*, 1977.
Inverness Field Club, (Editor Lorraine Maclean of Dochgarroch) *Loch Ness and Thereabouts*, 1991.
Nicholas Witchell, *Loch Ness and the Monster*, 1976.
Tim Dinsdale, *Loch Ness Monster*, 1961.
Richard Frere, *Loch Ness*, 1988.
E.A. Pratt, *Scottish Canals and Waterways*, 1922.
Duckworth and Langmuir, *West Highland Steamers*, 1967.
John Thomas, *The West Highland Railway*, David and Charles, 1965.
H.A. Vallance, *The Highland Railway*, 1963.

INTRODUCTION

Throughout the eighteenth century the natural gift of a massive geological fault, running diagonally across Scotland and already half full of water, attracted people to investigate making a canal through the Great Glen.

The local clans, oblivious to all this, continued to engage in a warlike series of Jacobite uprisings that lead indirectly and surprisingly to the construction of the canal. Initially the rebellions were followed by widespread depopulation and emigration from the Highlands. This went on unchecked for over fifty years before the Government of the day realised it had to do something to stop it and engaged Thomas Telford to survey for a canal. He was also to assess its value to the Navy in the wars with France and advise on whether it could be built by local labour thus stemming the tide of emigration.

Telford was the son of a shepherd from Dumfriesshire who, after an apprenticeship as a stone mason in Langholm, had made his name building roads and canals in England and Wales. He recommended a canal twenty foot deep, with locks of one hundred and sixty two foot by thirty eight foot (later enlarged to take 32 gun frigates and the largest ships engaged on the Baltic trade). He estimated that it would cost £350,000 and take seven years to build. And yes, it could be built with local labour (supervised by experienced engineers and craftsmen from the south!).

The Government approved Telford's plans and appointed Commissioners to oversee the project and disburse funds for what became the earliest state-funded transport undertaking in this country. It has remained in public ownership ever since and is now operated by British Waterways.

Work began in 1803. Telford and his engineers were operating well beyond the scope of anything that had been done before. As difficulties mounted, estimates of cost and completion dates were quickly surpassed. When the canal was finally opened in 1822 it had cost £840,000 to build, it was only fourteen feet deep, the French wars were over, the Baltic timber trade had collapsed and most ships were too big to use it. Despite having numerous critics this substandard, unfinished canal was too valuable to lose. Besides, the raised loch levels and diverted rivers would be difficult to reverse. So, the canal was closed again between 1844 and 1847 for substantial improvements and deepening.

Fishing boats were the principal commercial users and still use the canal today. Steamer services operated along the length of the canal and on Loch Ness until the Second World War. Pleasure cruising has been revived in recent years along with a thriving market in hire boats.

The rise in tourism is hardly surprising for a canal set in such spectacular scenery, rich in ruined castles and romanticism. For the waterborne tourist there is the added buzz that Nessie, the Loch Ness Monster, might just break surface and make the lucky photographer famous. In all this magnificence and mystery, it is easy to forget those early nineteenth century pioneers who moved mountains, raised lochs and changed the course, not just of rivers, but of history too. They were big men.

ACKNOWLEDGEMENTS

My introduction to the Caledonian Canal was in May 1983 when I took part in the Drambuie Loch Ness Marathon, a kind of rally event for nutters in inflatable boats. Despite the pain, I should thank Drambuie for the introduction. Without it I may never have realised how special this canal is.

I am grateful to a number of people who have helped in the preparation of this book. British Waterways for permission to use pictures on pages 7, 20, 49, 51 and inside back cover. and the staff, always cheerful and without whom there would be no story to tell. Janet Watson of Inverness Museum and Art Gallery for her assistance with historical information. The advice and help I received from Lorraine Maclean of Dochgarroch of the Inverness Field Club was invaluable as was that of Miss C.A. Goodfellow of Inverness Library and Fiona Marwick of the West Highland Museum, Fort William. Jim and Audrey Hogan of Caley Cruisers were a great help as were George Reid and Jimmy Munro whose memories were invaluable.

And my old friend Donald McKinnon who partnered me in that initial marathon, and came out of retirement for us to win in 1991. Hooray!

The aptly named *Mountaineer* sits below the looming bulk of Ben Nevis at the sea lock jetty. The lock was the southern, or western, terminal of the canal and was three miles northwest of Fort William at Corpach, on the shores of where Loch Linnhe and Loch Eil meet. In the lock, and partly obscured by the lockside shed, is the Glasgow to Inverness steamer *Cavalier*. If she was on schedule when this picture was taken, it was a Tuesday. The sea lock was opened in 1819 to allow vessels in to the basin to load and offload. It was enlarged in the 1960s as part of the development of the Corpach pulp mill, which has now sadly closed.

The basin was cut out of solid rock, its size limited by the slow progress of navvies having to do the work by hand. The engineers who contemplated such a task and the navvies who tackled it must have been brave men. One of the first things built for the canal at Corpach was a brewery to encourage those navvies to 'give up the pernicious habit of drinking whisky'. It seems however, that they continued to drink their whisky with the beer, possibly inventing that favourite Scottish tipple 'the hauf and a hauf. Between drinks they built a magnificent canal, starting with a pair of locks that lift the canal out of the basin and on to Banavie.

The poet Robert Southey, a friend of Telford's, described the immense flight of locks at Banavie as the greatest work of art in Britain. The locks, known as Neptune's Staircase, while not being art in the conventional sense are a tremendous achievement. In a quarter of a mile of continuous masonry, eight staircase locks raise the canal 62 feet. Staircase locks were cheaper and simpler to build than single ones, but they form bottlenecks because a large boat has to go all the way up the lock flight before another can come down. One solution is to put as many boats as possible through at one time, here observed by a party of Boy Scouts on a 1930s holiday rail tour known, quaintly, as a Scout Train Cruise.

Another solution, to provide basins in the middle of lock flights as passing places, is shown on early plans. They were not built at the time or in the 1840s when they were again rejected as too expensive. Despite the undoubted engineering achievement, some of the construction was not good and the locks had to be closed for repair on a number of occasions, as seen in this picture from the 1920s. Serious structural defects were exposed in 1929 by a sudden change in water pressure caused when a drifter, the *Girl Patricia*, smashed into the top gates. The gates of the top two locks collapsed, but the third set held, avoiding a catastrophic chain reaction down the whole flight.

The steamer terminal at Banavie Pier was at the top of the locks and traffic increased significantly when a short branch line linked it to the West Highland Railway, just in time for the tourist season of 1895. So, unlike other canals, the Caledonian benefitted from the coming of the railway. Passengers walked up the canal embankment from the station which was at a lower level than the pier. Waggons were shunted up a 1 in 24 gradient to a siding beside it, seen on the extreme left of this picture. When the Mallaig line was opened in 1901 a new Banavie station was constructed at the foot of the locks. Curiously, the name board on the old station was never changed, even though it was shown as Banavie Pier in timetables.

The whole section of canal, from Corpach up through Banavie and for the next few miles, is dominated by Ben Nevis, the highest mountain in Britain. It only achieved this status officially in 1870 when new measurements fixed its height at 4,406 feet. A weather observatory and even a hotel were built on the summit at one time. Today's tourists are climbers, who come in all seasons to face the challenges of the mountain, and walkers, who use the path to get to the top. Judging by the number of specialist shops in Fort William it has become a major industry together with the West Highland Way which spills a never ending stream of walkers and runners into the town to count their blisters and sponsorship money.

It seems remarkable that a canal in such mountainous country does not have the kind of majestic aqueducts that grace many smaller waterways. These, inaccurately named, Telfer Tunnels are the arches of the aqueduct over the Seangan Burn. One arch intended for farm carts is still used by motor vehicles to cross under the canal. This and the larger aqueduct at Glenloy are the most significant on the canal. But what the Caledonian may lack in quality is made up for by the sheer quantity of mountain streams that had to be culverted or diverted. The flow of rivers and burns, either culverted or feeding into the canal, was controlled by weirs to prevent structural damage while sumps and rock barriers stopped flood borne debris getting into the canal

The canal enters Loch Lochy at Gairlochy where a regulating lock to maintain water level differentials was built. It was always in danger of being overwhelmed by the huge volume of water in the loch and was swamped in 1834 when the outlet for the River Lochy was blocked after heavy rain. A second lock was built to reduce the danger and even this has had further flood defences added. The lock-keeper's house, to the left in this picture, is similar to one at Banavie. The first floor front room is named after Telford, who often stayed here. The bow front would have given him good views of the canal. Behind the houses is the River Lochy.

The Lochy was diverted at Gairlochy so that the first few hundred yards of canal could be cut on the river bed. The new course from Loch Lochy to the River Spean at Mucomir was used in later years to power a hydroelectric station. The Loch looks natural now, but the canal engineers manipulated nature on a staggering scale to raise its level by twelve feet. About three miles up the northern shore a wooded glen, known as The Dark Mile, leads to Loch Arkaig. It is steeped in Jacobite legend. Prince Charlie escaped through it after the Battle of Culloden and sheltered for a while in a cave there. D.K. Broster's trilogy of Jacobite books *The Flight of the Heron* and *The Gleam in the North* was concluded by *The Dark Mile*, named after the glen.

While Prince Charlie hid on the northern shore, the military road on the south would have been busy with his enemies. There was a Kings House near the top end of the loch at Letterfinlay. It became an inn in less turbulent times and an extremely bad one, according to accounts of early travellers in Scotland who rated it as one of the worst in the country. Travellers today will find it much improved. The canal leaves Loch Lochy by the Laggan Locks, a staircase pair where serious cracks in the lock walls closed the canal for almost all of 1976. A hundred years earlier it was closed for three months after the steamer *Staffa* rammed the top gates. Hundreds of clansmen were killed at Laggan in 1544, in a terrible battle between MacDonalds and Frasers. Only a handful lived through the carnage, but the conflict is remembered more because, in the heat of that July day, the men took off their shirts and fought half naked.

Clearly this canal felt it had little to fear from the railways and sold space to them on its advertising hoardings. MacBraynes steamers promoted circular tours too, with railway journeys returning passengers south from Inverness by way of Aberdeen and the east coast.

Itinerant entertainers performed at some lock sides for the benefit of steamer passengers. It was a busker's dream a captive audience even if there were only two boats per day. Inevitably there was a piper, though this one at Gairlochy isn't wearing a kilt and seems to be only the accompaniment to the wee dancer.

Paddy was another lockside entertainer. His name, style of dress and the shillelagh he is holding in the picture postcard would suggest he was Irish. That a picture postcard was printed of him suggests he was well known. He appears to have plied his trade beside Laggan Locks for many years. In the 1898 photograph he is seen performing with a wee boy, who seems to be able to play the flute and dance at the same time. He could have been a young man when the postcard was published, which may explain his absence. Unless, of course, Paddy had heard about the old showbiz maxim of never appearing with animals or children.

East of Laggan Locks the canal enters Laggan Avenue, a private world where the bare hillsides and mountain vistas are replaced by great mature pine trees flanking the canal on both sides. These plantations are really quite narrow, but viewed from the canal they look as if they go on for ever. The trees also disguise a deep cutting, which was excavated to a depth that allowed a dredger to float in from Loch Oich and finish the job. The scale of the cutting is emphasised about two thirds of the way along the avenue by a massive elevated weir which feeds Allt-an-Lagain into the canal. In wet weather the water roars into its sump, disturbing the peace of this tranquil place. When it is dry an apology for a mighty stream trickles over the edge.

Laggan Bridge spans the canal where it enters Loch Oich. The original double leaf cast iron bridge was replaced by a massive swing bridge in 1932 when the whole road through the Great Glen was improved. Loch Oich is the smallest of the three main lochs that make up the canal and its wooded shores and islands make it quite different from the others. It forms the summit of the canal at 106 feet above sea level. Telford abandoned plans to run the canal, with a towpath, along the southern shore. Instead he dredged a channel through the centre of the shallow loch using two of the earliest steam bucket dredgers. Navigation in the narrow channel was always going to be difficult for unpowered craft and an early painting shows a sailing ship being towed through the loch by a rowing boat!

At the southern end of the loch is the attractive Great Glen Water Park, where holiday chalets can be rented and boats hired. But it was not always peaceful here. Returning from France in 1663, after their father's death, the two sons of the chief of the MacDonnell's of Keppoch were murdered by seven kinsmen left in charge by the old chief. Clansmen loyal to the sons then killed and decapitated the seven. They washed the severed heads in a stream and presented them to the MacDonnell of Glengarry. History does not record his reaction but two hundred years later his descendant erected a monument beside the stream. It is probably the only one in the world to an act of treachery and vengeance. The stream had become known as the Well of the Seven Heads.

The MacDonnell of Glengarry was, in 1745, a leading Jacobite sympathiser. After the Battle of Culloden, his stronghold, Invergarry Castle, was destroyed by Government troops in retribution for the help he had given Bonnie Prince Charlie. His descendant lived in a mansion near the ruin, overlooking Loch Oich. Whatever this new Glengarry's sympathies were, they were not for the canal, He disliked its threat to his privacy, objected when Telford was unable to screen it behind a wooded embankment and demanded an additional bridge over the Laggan Cut. He prevented work in places and on one occasion 'held up' the workmen and stole a boat. Yet despite these differences he was an honoured guest at the opening ceremony in 1822 which he attended with all due ceremony befitting a Highland chief and gentleman.

Before marching south, Bonnie Prince Charlie mustered his army at Aberchalder at the north end of Loch Oich. The more prosaic canal builders diverted the River Oich over a weir to maintain the level of the loch. This bridge over the river, in the small picture, was built as part of the road improvements in the Glen in the 1930s and replaced a delicate looking suspension bridge. Most of the canal bridges were replaced at the same time and the stone supports for the old Laggan and Aberchalder bridges can still be seen. The long picture shows the only original bridge left, at Moy west of Gairlochy. The problem of opening both halves of these bridges was solved by bridge keepers rowing a boat across the canal to open the second half. Presumably the road improvements did away with the rowing boats too.

Two single locks and three secret miles take the canal down from Loch Oich to Fort Augustus. Cullochy Lock is close enough to be seen from Aberchalder Bridge, but the isolated Kytra Lock is hidden in the hills. Its only links with the outside world are the canal itself and a mile and a half of rough road to Fort Augustus. In winter it must seem remote, but in summer it looks idyllic with passing boats and a holiday cottage on the other side of the lock. Steamers took enough time to go through the locks at Kytra and Fort Augustus for passengers to walk between them and enjoy a lovely 'natural' scene where the canal, following the original course of the River Oich, has been allowed to fill the base of low rocky tree-clad hills, creating magical little inlets and islands.

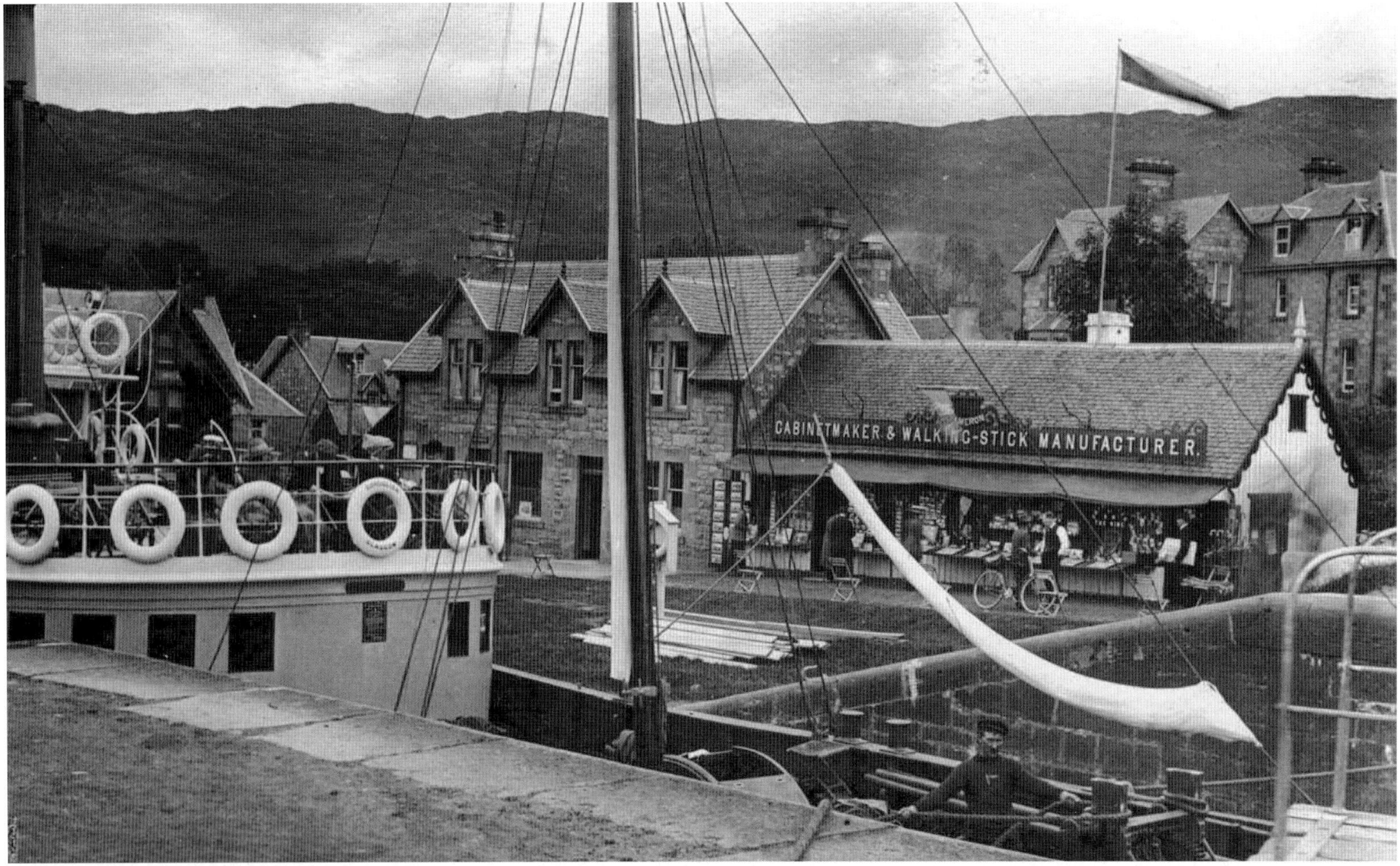

Fort Augustus was originally a village called Killihuimen. After the Jacobite uprisings of 1715 and 1719 it became a garrison town and was renamed in honour of William Augustus, Duke of Cumberland. The canal imposed itself more peacefully and the passage of boats through the locks was obviously a big event. It brought excitement for the locals, business for traders and a welcome break ashore for steamer passengers. They could visit the imposing Abbey and school, belonging to the Benedictine monks and view the remains of the fort in the Abbey grounds. In this otherwise unremarkable little town, the only other attraction mentioned in MacBrayne's guidebook of 1893, was John MacDonald's shop beside the locks. It was noted for Highland crooks!

The intrepid Mr Cameron however had other ideas. His shop was adjacent to MacDonald's, but that clearly wasn't going to stop him luring passengers away from the other attractions and into his, small but well-placed, canalside emporium. Apart from being an unlikely combination of walking stick (crook) manufacturer and cabinetmaker he appears to have sold just about everything else too, particularly that ubiquitous Edwardian souvenir and principal means of communication, the picture postcard. Some pictures in this book will no doubt have come from Mr Cameron's shop; and Mr MacDonald's too.

The flight of locks is the most conspicuous feature in this view of the town from the Abbey tower. The construction of the five locks was poor and they had to be rebuilt in 1837 after one collapsed. There was further trouble in 1882 when the steamer *Rockabill* ran into a lock gate and closed the canal for eight days. Stone for building the locks came from a rock cutting used to divert the River Oich from its meandering course. This allowed the canal to be aligned to enter Loch Ness down the last few hundred yards of the original river bed. The river can be seen to the right of the picture with the viaduct of the ill-fated Invergarry and Fort Augustus Railway crossing it.

The Highland Railway Company resisted all attempts to push a railway up the Great Glen to Inverness, but despite bitter legal battles they couldn't stop this one getting halfway there. But it was always going to struggle. It went through an empty landscape from one small community at Spean Bridge to another at Fort Augustus. It was extended over the canal and the river to a new pier on Loch Ness. Extravagant construction and the purchase of ground for a double track left no money to operate it (let alone get to Inverness) so from 1903 to 1907 it was worked by the Highland. Passengers however still preferred the canal steamers and after only three years the extension over the canal was closed. The North British Railway operated the line for a while. It was closed, saved again and closed finally in 1946, possibly the only railway to be put out of business by a canal.

The best known steamer on the canal was David MacBrayne's *Gondolier*. She was built in 1866 and started operating a daily service between Banavie and Inverness. She shared the route, first with *Glengarry* and then, from 1895, with *Gairlochy*. They started at each end, passed in the middle on Loch Oich and repeated the trip the other way the following day throughout the tourist season. She was taken off in 1939, but her fate was sealed early in the Second World War when a German submarine sank HMS *Royal Oak* at her moorings in the Orkney naval base of Scapa Flow. Anxious to avoid a repetition, the Admiralty sank 'block ships' to close the gaps between the islands, *Gondolier* was one of these, sunk in Water Sound between the islands of Burray and South Ronaldsay in 1940.

This picture, from 1898, shows passengers enjoying the delights of a bracing promenade on the top deck of *Gondolier*. Well wrapped up against the wind and weather in their heavy tweeds, plus fours and spats they are the very epitome of the wealthy Victorian holidaymaker. The fitting out of the boat is interesting too with upholstered seat cushions on the bench seating along the railing not perhaps what you would expect in wet and windy Scotland. Unless, of course, you were a wealthy Victorian holidaymaker.

David MacBrayne advertised his sailings from Glasgow to Inverness as *The Royal Route*. This involved taking a steamer from Glasgow or Gourock to Ardrishaig, travelling along the Crinan Canal on his little steamer *Linnet* and joining another steamer at Crinan for Corpach. An 'omnibus' took passengers from Corpach to Banavie Pier where they joined one of the canal steamers. The route got its name because Queen Victoria had travelled through the Crinan in 1847 and both Prince Albert in 1847 and herself in 1873 had gone through the Caledonian. Apparently, she found canal travel tedious.

The oldest of the paddle steamers was *Glengarry*. She was built in 1844 as the *Edinburgh Castle* for the Holy Loch service on the Clyde, but was transferred to the canal two years later. She was renamed in 1875. When she was replaced on the Banavie run she continued along with another small steamer *Lochness* on the mail route between Inverness and Fort Augustus. In the 1920s she was apparently still on this run and returned to the Banavie run during the summer. In December 1927 she was withdrawn from service and scrapped, but not forgotten because her wheel was preserved as an exhibit by Inverness Museum.

Another regular on the canal between 1883 and 1919 was MacBrayne's *Cavalier*. She was a cargo boat, but had 'First Class sleeping accommodation' for passengers too, although meals were optional. She left Glasgow for Inverness every Monday and took a week for the round trip. She was, of course, able to navigate the Caledonian Canal, but was too big for the Crinan Canal and had to go round the Mull of Kintyre. Being a deep sea, screw-propelled boat, her high sides and lack of paddle boxes mark her out from the other canal and loch steamers.

The boat observed here by our Victorian tourists, below the Fort Augustus locks, is the tug *Scot*. She was built in 1876 and succeeded in 1931 by another tug, also called *Scot*. She in turn was replaced by another tug, *Scot II* (!) in 1937. This third *Scot* was converted by British Waterways in 1961 to take passengers on cruises from Inverness to Loch Ness, thus reviving the cruising tradition that, apart from a couple of brief ventures in the 1940s and 1950s, had lain dormant since the demise of *Gondolier*. Scot II has since been withdrawn, while newer, privately owned vessels have elevated loch cruising to a different level of comfort and sophistication.

The Loch Ness mail steamers used Inveroich Pier at the mouth of the canal at Fort Augustus. This avoided the need to negotiate the locks or perform the impossible and reverse down the channel. The steamer at the pier is *Lochness* (yes it is all one word) which operated on Loch Ness between 1885 and 1929. One of the other steamers, *Gairlochy*, made a dramatic exit from the scene when she was completely burnt out at Fort Augustus on Christmas Eve 1919. Traffic had declined after the First World War and her unexpected demise may have pre-empted the inevitable. Her hulk can still be seen behind the pier when the loch is low.

Having advised a nervous government in London that support still existed for another Jacobite uprising, Major General George Wade was instructed to put a 'military vessel' or galley, on Loch Ness, repair Fort William and build new forts at Fort Augustus and Inverness. More importantly he was to improve communications between them. His roads and bridges through the Great Glen began a process, continued by the canal, of 'opening up the Highlands'. His work inspired the old rhyme: 'If you'd seen the road before it was made, you'd bless the name of General Wade'. The Abbey at Fort Augustus now occupies the site and little of the fort remains. Here *Gondolier* heads out of the canal past the Abbey, Inveroich pier and the foreground hulk of *Gairlochy*.

With the Railway Companies at each others' throats there was never going to be a railway between Fort Augustus and Inverness and with only indifferent roads lochside communities relied on the steamers. There were piers at Invermoriston. Foyers, Inverfarigaig, Aldourie, Abriachan and Drumnadrochit which was served by Temple Pier, seen here, on the north side of Urquhart Bay. The canal made Loch Ness a busy waterway. The first hydroelectric plant in Britain was built at Foyers. It was to power an aluminium smelter sited there to take advantage of plentiful and cheap power and access to the sea. Steamers stopping at Foyers allowed passengers time to inspect the dramatic waterfalls and any poets in the company felt obliged to pen an appropriate eulogy as Rabbie Burns had done before them.

The natural site and commanding presence of Castle Urquhart have ensured Loch Ness and the Great Glen their full share of Scotland's troubles, from the iron age to the Jacobite rebellions. English troops occupied it in 1292 and it changed hands a number of times during the Scottish Wars of Independence. It continued to change hands as inter-clan warfare took place amidst wider struggles for power. It was a Clan Grant stronghold when Montrose won his famous victory at Inverlochy and it was still in Grant hands when Cromwell had a galley built in Inverness and hauled to Loch Ness to quell the turbulent Highlanders. After the restoration of the monarchy, William of Orange deposed James VII and in the unrest that followed the castle's garrison blew it up to prevent it falling into Jacobite hands.

Claims that the Loch Ness Monster used the canal to get from the sea into the loch are as unlikely as the claims that this fresh water loch, fifty feet above the sea, is somehow linked to it by a subterranean passage. Loch Ness is deeper than the North Sea being for much of its length 700 feet and in places 900 hundred feet deep. It is twenty four miles long, up to a mile and a half wide and has a surface area of thirty five square miles. The water maintains a constant (cold) temperature, but never freezes. The estimated volume of 263,000,000,000 cubic feet makes the loch the largest body of fresh water in the British Isles, greater than all the lakes and reservoirs of England and Wales put together. So, if there is a monster. Loch Ness is big enough for it and its family to live there undetected. Some of the surrounding mountains enter the water so steeply they form sheer underwater cliffs, overhangs and numerous 'des res' for monsters.

Legend tells of Saint Columba seeing a water horse in the River Ness in 565 AD and there are other stories of sightings from later centuries. In the 1930s however, Nessie was brought immutably into the public eye when the new main road was built along the northern shore of the loch. The clearance of trees also cleared the view. The Inverness Courier reported a sighting in 1933 by Mr Alex Campbell, a water bailiff, from Fort Augustus. In 1934 Mr R.K. Wilson, a London surgeon, took a now famous photograph of the monster's head and neck. Other important sightings date from 1945 and another 'classic' photograph was taken in 1955 by a Mr McNab of West Kilbride. The monster couldn't be ignored. Even the Italian Air Force claimed to have killed it during the Second World War.

Another sighting in June 1933 confounded even the most ardent believer. A Mr and Mrs Spicer from London were driving between Inverfarigaig and Dores when 'a most extraordinary form of animal' crossed the road in front of them. When they reached the spot all that they could see was a gap in the bushes. Land sightings are rare, but sufficient to encourage stories of monsters coming ashore to steal lambs; bad news for lambs, good news for postcard publishers. It wasn't long before people arrived to investigate and one of the first, a Commander Gould R.N., questioned the Spicers. The first serious expedition was organised by Sir Edward Mountain, an insurance magnate. Twenty men kept a dawn to dusk surveillance of the loch throughout July 1934. They failed to obtain that vital piece of evidence and it was to be thirty years before other attempts were made.

Tim Dinsdale filmed a disturbance in the loch in 1960 which was later analysed and declared 'animate'. Serious Nessie hunting began in 1961 when the Loch Ness Investigation Bureau was set up. They observed the loch for the next twelve summers and carried out underwater experiments with sonar and submarines. In 1972 a team from the Academy of Applied Science of Boston, working with the Bureau and using sonar and an underwater stroboscopic camera photographed the monster at close quarters. The pictures, taken in murky, peat-coloured water were computer enhanced to improve clarity and one appeared to show a diamond-shaped flipper. Photographs in later years were claimed to show a swimming monster and a close up of a head. Despite all this, the Official Loch Ness Monster Exhibition at Drumnadrochit takes a neutral line, leaving the visitor to decide if the evidence is conclusive. I did!

It is hardly surprising that a record breaking loch should attract other record breakers. The most famous was John Cobb who came to the loch in 1952 to add the world water speed record to His land speed record. The attempt ended in tragedy when his boat, *Crusader* hit turbulence in the water and crashed, killing him instantly. A memorial to him has been erected beside the loch. For others it's the loch itself that presents the challenge. Brenda Sherrat became the first person to swim its length when she was eighteen. Others have followed, but few have had the impact of George Parsonage whose record of 2 hours, 43 minutes and 34.1 seconds, for rowing between the Fort Augustus and Bona Ferry lights, stood for many years until he and Peter Haining sped down the loch in 2 hours, 28 minutes, and 9 seconds in April 1993. Despite this feat George (right) is better known for his life saving exploits on the River Clyde and Peter (left) for winning the world lightweight sculls championship in 1993, 1994 and 1995.

Fishing boats dry their nets beside the Bona Ferry lighthouse, while waiting, perhaps, for a favourable wind or a tug to tow them down the loch. A bay window at the front of the (otherwise domestic) lighthouse was used as the original light to mark the exit from Loch Ness at Bona Ferry. This is now supplemented by additional lights and a lit and buoyed channel to guide shipping through the narrows and into Loch Dochfour. Bona was on a road that ran south from Beauly to a ford over the Ness, east of where the lighthouse is now. It was guarded by a castle with a grim history, even by the standards of these parts. The crossing was used by drovers, cattle thieves and even fugitives from the Battle of Culloden. It was very busy before the canal was dredged and the lochs raised, so ferry piers were provided by the Canal Commissioners, presumably as compensation for the loss of the local amenity.

The River Ness now flows out of Loch Dochfour over a 600 yard long weir near Dochgarroch regulating lock. At times the change of water level at the lock can be very small between canal and loch. All the canal lock gates are now operated by a hydraulic mechanism, but originally they were worked by capstans, like this one at Dochgarroch being pushed round by two men, a boy and a dog. It took seven revolutions to open the gates and seven to close them, so a complete locking operation involving all four gates would require the (presumably dizzy) lock-keepers, boat crews or dogs, to run round in circles fifty six times. This spectacle apparently amused Queen Victoria, forgetting for a moment her dislike of canal travel.

Like the other major rivers, the Ness was diverted to make room for the canal. The embankment between the two was planted with whin and broom to stabilise it, but it leaked badly. To cure the problem, huge pieces of specially woven woollen cloth were laid on the bed of the canal and impregnated with clay puddle. It was unconventional and it stopped the leaks. But alas, sailing an open boat over the woolly blanket does not feel any warmer. A warm glow may have come over the navvy who found a solid silver chain, thought to be of Pictish origin, in 1808 at the base of Torvean Hill (where this picture was taken from). It was bought from him by an Inverness jeweller who presented it to the National Museum of Antiquities in Edinburgh.

Gaelic scholars disagree on the meaning of Tomnahurich. Some say it is the 'hill of the yew trees', while others prefer 'knoll of the earth'. Either way the canal passes this distinctive hill on its way into Inverness, bringing to pass the prediction of the seventeenth century Highland prophet, the Brahan Seer, that one day full-rigged ships would be seen sailing inland behind it; as this picture of full rigged fishing boats passing Tomnahurich Bridge shows. The old bridge was replaced in 1937 by a swing bridge designed by the engineers Crouch and Hogg. A site adjacent to the bridge became the operating base for Jacobite Cruises when their trip boats started sailing in 1975.

The base for the old paddle steamers was at Burnfoot near Muirtown. The outside of a bend here was widened in the 1840s to create a place to turn the steamers above Muirtown locks. Turning points, known as winding holes, are common on smaller canals and were perhaps thought unnecessary on the Caledonian, but the bottlenecks of the lock flights must have caused a re-think. Burnfoot was also the base where the steamers were overhauled and laid up for the winter. Major repair and slipping however, was carried out at Thornbush on the River Ness. The steamers can be seen behind the line of fishing boats which went through the canal in great numbers at certain times of the year — to keep up with migrating shoals of herring. Today Burnfoot is the base for the oldest fleet of hire cruisers on the canal, a boat-building yard and one of the largestest chandleries in Scotland.

The steamer wharf at Muirtown was, like Banavie, at the top of a flight of locks. The arrival of a steamer was a big moment. Passengers would be greeted by a line of hotel omnibuses and there was great competition amongst the drivers to see who could hustle most passengers into their bus. Perhaps too there was competition amongst the passengers to be first off the boat and onto the bus of their favoured hotel, which may explain why they have congregated on the one side of *Gondolier* making her heel over so alarmingly.

Of the hotels featured in this picture of the waiting omnibuses, the Royal was advertised in Mackenzie's 1896 *Guide to Inverness* as '… being the nearest first class hotel to Post and Telegraph offices and the New Golf Course'. The Station was proud of being 'Patronised by their Royal Highnesses the Prince and Princess of Wales and other members of the Royal Family and most of the Nobility of Europe'. The Caledonian boasted '... a magnificent Ladies Drawing Room overlooking the River Ness', while the Imperial had '… excellent commercial and stock rooms. And hot and cold baths!' The Palace contented itself by being '… nearest to the canal steamers'; a useful advantage when they left at seven in the morning.

Not all of the passengers carried by the steamers were travelling from one place to another, some took to the water as part of an excursion, like this jolly crowd enjoying the Howe of the Mearns trip to Loch Ness on 6 August 1909. Exchanging the rolling landscape and red earth of the countryside, so vividly described by Lewis Grassic Gibbon in his famous novel *Sunset Song*, they must have got up early in the morning, travelled to Inverness by train, sailed round the loch on board the steamer *Lochness* and returned, all in the one day. This picture, taken to record their memorable trip, was used as a postcard by someone from Drumlithie.

Tall-masted, square-riggers were probably thought to be a thing of the past until many, like these, sailed through the canal in 1991 during the Cutty Sark Tall Ships Race. Like their predecessors they used the canal in preference to sailing round the top of Scotland and through the unpredictable Pentland Firth. There are four locks in the Muirtown flight. At the bottom, the swing bridge divides confined canal from the extensive Muirtown basin. The Commissioners had planned a brewery at this end of the canal too, to wean the navvies off whisky, but abandoned the idea and ironically two distilleries were eventually built at the basin. Little else in the way of industry was attracted to the area, unless you count Inverness Caledonian Football Club, possibly the only team in the country to take its name from a canal, although that was partly changed when the club moved away from the Muirtown area.

It was not until the First World War that predictions about the canal's usefulness in wartime were fulfilled, when considerable numbers of Admiralty vessels used the canal but the increased traffic was no 'bonanza' as the Navy was exempt from paying dues. U.S. Naval Base 18 was established at Muirtown basin. From here the American Navy took part in laying the minefield known as the Northern Barrage. It stretched from Orkney to Norway and was designed to keep German submarines out of the Atlantic. The mines and sinkers were shipped across the Atlantic to Corpach where they were loaded into lighters for the journey through the canal. Buoys and navigation lights were installed so that the operation could go on round the clock.

Muirtown basin is massive and if it took bravery to cut the Corpach basin out of rock it took stamina to dig this twenty acre basin, 800 yards long by 140 yards wide. Telford planned it as a second harbour for Inverness, but boats quickly became too big and it never achieved its potential. The basin ends at Clachnaharry Works Lock where the initial construction was co-ordinated from. British Waterways still have their workshops here, though they have moved their offices to the other side of the basin. Lock gates made here were transported to site and installed by the strange looking vessel in this picture called (you've guessed it!) *Gatelifter*. A little display here describes Telford's other mountain canal, the Gota in Sweden, which is twinned with the Caledonian.

Crossing the canal and towpath in the foreground of this view from Clachnaharry Works Lock is the railway heading north out of Inverness. Originally known as the Inverness and Ross-shire Railway, construction began on 19 September 1860 when Lady Matheson, wife of Sir Alexander Matheson of Ardross, the driving force behind the building of the line, dug the first spadeful of earth. The first section to Dingwall, including the swing bridge over the canal, was opened in June 1862. The line became part of the Highland Railway when that company was incorporated in 1865, and it was progressively pushed north eventually reaching Wick and Thurso in 1874. A branch line to Muirtown Basin was also opened in 1877. The lock-keeper's house for the sea lock can be seen in the distance, above the gates across the towpath.